**Essential Question**
Why are rules important?

# Government RULES

by Anton Wilson

**Chapter 1**
Rules Protect Us. . . . . . . . . . . . . . . . . . . 2

**Chapter 2**
Food Rules. . . . . . . . . . . . . . . . . . . . . 5

**Chapter 3**
Animal Rules. . . . . . . . . . . . . . . . . . . . 10

**Chapter 4**
Idea Rules . . . . . . . . . . . . . . . . . . . . . 12

**Respond to Reading** . . . . . . . . . . . . . . 15

**PAIRED READ** Pool Rules . . . . . . . . . . . . . . . . 16

**Glossary/Index** . . . . . . . . . . . . . . . . . 19

**Focus on Social Studies** . . . . . . . . . . 20

# Chapter 1
# Rules Protect Us

The government makes rules to keep people safe.

Rules are important. They help keep us safe. They help us get along with each other. Following the rules can make life better.

Parents make rules for a family. Schools make rules for students. Our government makes rules, too.

People visit a geyser known as "Old Faithful" in Yellowstone National Park.

## National Parks

National parks are public places. They are all over the country. Yellowstone was the first one. It became a national park in 1872. Mountains, rivers, lakes, and forests form this park.

This park is in Tennessee and North Carolina.

Now the United States has almost 400 national parks. Some are set in nature. Others are important to our history. Rules protect these places. The rules will make sure the parks are around for a long time.

What have you learned about national parks?

4

Marvin Dembinsky Photo Associates/Alamy

# Chapter 2
# Food Rules

This stamp tells you the meat was checked.

The government has rules about the food you eat. These rules help keep foods from making people sick. The government checks some foods such as meat and eggs. If these foods are safe, they get a stamp.

Eating well helps you learn at school.

## School Lunches

Schools follow rules about food. They serve food that was checked. The government gives schools food and money. Some schools serve free lunches to children.

## Food Safety

The government helps people learn about food safety. Some foods are unsafe if they are eaten raw. The government explains how to cook food safely. Following rules for cooking food can save lives!

Food packages show rules about how to cook meat.

## How to Store Eggs Safely

| Type of egg | Can be refrigerated for | Can be frozen for |
|---|---|---|
| raw egg | 3–5 weeks (in shell) | 1 year (out of shell) |
| hard-boiled egg | 1 week | do not freeze |
| store-bought eggnog | 3–5 days | 6 months |

The government tells us how to safely store and serve food. The chart shows how long to keep eggs. Some rules explain how hot meat should get before we can eat it.

## Medicines

The government has rules about medicines. Medicines have to be tested. Then the government may **approve** a medicine. Finally stores can sell the medicine. It is safe to use.

**STOP AND CHECK**

Why does the government make rules for foods and medicines?

These people learn how to take their medicine.

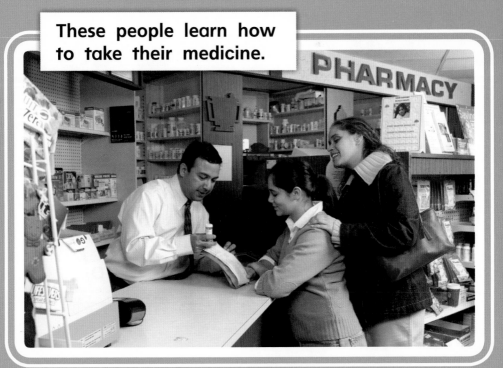

# Chapter 3
# Animal Rules

There are rules for fishing.

What protects animals? Rules do. The government has rules about hunting and fishing. These rules help both animals and people. People who break a rule must pay a fine.

Photodisc Collection/Getty Images

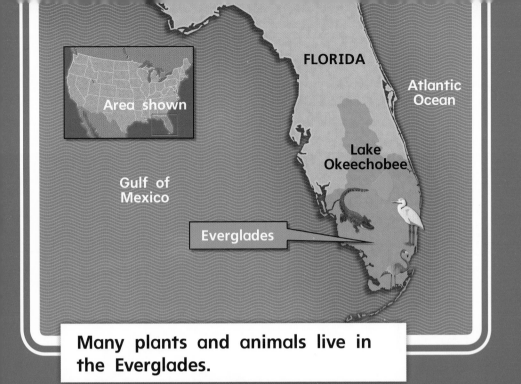

Many plants and animals live in the Everglades.

An animal can't tell people how to behave. But our government can! Government rules protect places where animals live. People who visit must follow the rules. Even people who own land must follow rules about how they use it.

Illustration: Rob Schuster

**STOP AND CHECK**

Why does the government have rules to protect nature?

# Chapter 4
# Idea Rules

A copyright page appears near the front of a book.

Some government rules protect ideas. **Copyright** rules say that nobody can copy ideas in a book. When a writer first exclaimed, "I have an idea!" he or she probably didn't think about copyright! But these rules help writers.

The TM on the box means "trademark."
No one else can use this cereal name.

## Patents

Other rules protect inventors.
Inventors get a patent to protect
their ideas. A patent is a paper that
says the inventor came up with the
idea.

**Many items in your home have patents.**

Patents say that no one can make, use, or sell another person's invention. This rule can help people with good ideas.

Government rules help improve our lives. They protect our rights. They keep us safe and healthy. We can help each other if we all follow the rules.

**STOP AND CHECK**

Why would an inventor want a patent?

# Respond to Reading

## Summarize

Use details to help you summarize *Government Rules.*

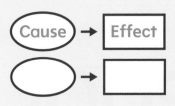

## Text Evidence

1. How do you know *Government Rules* is expository text? Genre

2. What caused the government to create rules about food? Cause and Effect

3. Use your knowledge of multiple-meaning words to tell the meaning of *fine* on page 10. Multiple-Meaning Words

4. Why is it important to have rules that protect national parks? Text to World

**Compare Texts**
Read about why pool rules are important.

# POOL RULES

Do you enjoy swimming? Pools are fun in hot weather. Many pools have the same rules. These rules are on signs. That way everyone can see them.

Many cities have public pools.

16

# Diving

Some pools are deep. There may be a diving board. But it is against the rules to dive in **shallow** water. The "No Diving" rule helps people stay safe.

# Running

The area around a pool is wet and slippery. The "No Running" rule reminds people to walk carefully.

# Eating and Drinking

Food and drinks are not allowed in the pool. The water could get dirty. People could slip if food is dropped.

Glass bottles might break. People could cut their bare feet.

Follow the rules at the pool. You will stay safe and have fun!

## Make Connections
What important rule do you follow? Why? Essential Question

How are government rules and pool rules alike? Text to Text

# Glossary

**approve** *(uh-PROOV)* to accept something or say it is good *(page 9)*

**copyright** *(KOP-ee-right)* legal ownership of something you have written that you can make money from *(page 12)*

**shallow** *(SHAL-oh)* not deep *(page 17)*

# Index

cooking food, *7–8*

diving board, *17*

fishing, *10*

patent, *13–14*

United States, *4*

# Focus on
# Social Studies

**Purpose** To find out why classroom rules are important

## What to Do

**Step 1** ▶ Write down two classroom rules.

**Step 2** ▶ Write down how each rule helps your class. Use a chart like this.

| Rule | How It Helps |
|------|--------------|
|      |              |
|      |              |

**Step 3** ▶ Compare your chart with a partner's chart.